KINGDOM WORSHIP

The Universal Symphony of
Effectual Praise

[signature]
7/18/15

DR. VICTOR T. NYARKO

OTHER EXCITING BOOKS BY DR. VICTOR T. NYARKO

DIVINE EMPOWERMENT

This book is an exposition on the power of the efficacious blood of Jesus Christ, the legacy and empowerment it provided for the first Apostles, for today's believer in Jesus Christ, and for all who will come after.

It reveals the resources that God through Christ has made available and at our disposal for the successful accomplishment of the great commission. It also teaches the reader, how one can tap into these resources by believing it, claiming it and possessing it.

ISBN 978-1484879832

A DISCONNECTED GENERATION

This book presents striking differences between the generation of Moses and the generation of Joshua. Although Joshua's generation witnessed a glimpse of the miracles and wonder workings of God, they lacked a personal relationship with the God of their fathers and the God of Israel.
ISBN 1-59330-075-1

DEALING WITH REJECTION

Rejection of one kind or another is inevitable throughout ones' life; therefore any tool that can be acquired to help deal with it should be a welcome choice. In this book, Dr. Nyarko presents the key elements that lead to the feeling of rejection and how to cope with rejection from a biblical perspective.
ISBN 1-59330-471-4

BEAUTY FOR ASHES

I t has been the church's tradition to think that great revival could be sparked by extensive advertising, putting up the right preacher and playing the right music. If these are true ingredients for revival, then John the Baptist' revival which ignited and blazed a trail in the desolate and obscure wilderness of Judea wouldn't have had the impact it did. On the contrary, out of the ashes of repentance come revival, refreshing, restitution and restoration.

ISBN 1-59330-605-9

WHERE ARE THE FATHERS

The lack of fathers at home has been one of society's greatest dilemmas of our time. This book has a timely word from the Lord for everyone. God our father is calling all fathers through the pen of this godly author and father, back to the honorable and critical role of fatherhood. Get ready, Read it, Repent and pass it on.

ISBN 13: 9781593302436

Available online and at your local Christian Bookstore. For more information email Dr. Nyarko at victoryfamily@verizon.net.

DEDICATION

To my lovely wife Joan Elaine,
and our incredible special gifts
from the Lord –
Tori, Vanya and Joash.

TABLE OF CONTENTS

PREFACE

The inspiration for this book first came to me as a result of how well a series of messages I preached at Victory Family Worship Center on 'Kingdom Worship' was received. Consequently, the command "Praise ye the Lord" has taken on new meaning and response in Victory Family Worship Center. I therefore felt the need to share this revelation in God's word with a broader audience since there is obviously the need for todays' church to understand elements which constitute effectual praise and worship.

It has been my observation, from the numerous church events and conferences that I have been honored to be invited to participate in, either as a guest speaker or in some other role or capacity, that many of the younger generation within our congregations are disengaged when it comes to worship. Many of them do not actively participate in the praise and worship experience of the church. I have noticed through the many churches I have visited that many of our young people are totally disconnected from the worship experience in our Christian liturgical or public worship services.

I have been in services that while praise and worship is in full gear, one would find that several young people totally lost in the on-going worship experience. One would most often find that some have their eyes widely opened and are disengaged in what is going on around them, as if they are in some sort of wonderland. They are often seen either staring around or they pre-occupy themselves with some form of distraction so as to sustain them through the period of worship.

To many, worship has become a designated role of the worship team or worship leader. As a result they end up becoming either the audience being entertained by good gospel music or simply spectators of what's going on during worship. In other words, there is a general lack of interest and full involvement in the worship experience in most of our churches.

It's worth noting that although praising God is not the same as worshipping him, the two words *praise* and *worship* has been deliberately used interchangeably in this book in order to underscore the significance and inter-relationship between both words and how critical they are to the spiritual life of the believer.

My goal for writing this book is to share with the Body of Christ, the central role and significance that praise and worship plays in our modern day liturgical or public worship. I would therefore invite you to fasten your seatbelt and take an expository journey with me into the pages of scriptures in order to find out what it really means to praise God, where God ought to be praised and how God ought to be praised.

ACKNOWLEDGMENTS

I am grateful to my one and only lovely wife Joan and to our beautiful children Victoria, Joash and Vanya for their patience and sacrifices, which enable me to fulfill my calling in serving the Lord and his church universal. Often times it seems as if I live at the church and sleep at home, considering the amount of hours spent each week on the church premises. When I am not at home, they know exactly where to find me, so again I say thanks to my family for all your support and understanding.

I am indebted to my Executive Pastoral Assistant, Stephanie Eccles, whose diligence and dedication has freed me from the numerous church administrative tasks that used to occupy a great deal of my time. "Free at last, free at last, thank God I'm free". I'm freed up to pray more, and to study God's word more than ever before.

To my chief editor, Andrea Williams under whose scrutiny, this book and every other book I have written has gone through. Her abilities are such a great gift to the body of Christ. Thanks Sister Angie.

To Dean Harvey for the superb work done in designing such an awesome book cover. Brother Dean is indeed a great talent to the body of Christ.

My sincere thanks to all the Princes and Princesses of God's royal province at Victory Family Worship Center, and to the churches within the New York Metro District UPCI and beyond, whose hunger and thirst for the infallible word of God has driven me to spend several hours weekly to study God's word in my little bible study laboratory in the Bronx.

Above all, I would like to acknowledge the prompting and guidance of the Holy Spirit of God through the hours spent in prayer and research towards the writing of this book.

It is my prayer that this book will be a blessing to pastors, churches, worship leaders, and believers alike in God's Kingdom across the globe. This book will revolutionize your understanding of worship for the betterment of God's Kingdom on earth. To God be all the glory.

INTRODUCTION

I chose the title, *Kingdom Worship* because worship, unlike many Kingdom activities, is central to the call of every believer. King Solomon in all his wisdom declared that; *"The whole duty of man is to fear God and obey his commandment"*. Worship is therefore a duty and not an option. It is mandatory for the child of God, whether or not he or she wants to. It is an experience and not an act. Praise and Worship transcends the realm of the physical or where humans exist. It has its footprints from heaven and it's a prototype of what eternity is going to be like. It is the nature of the main activity that the redeemed of the Lord will be engaged in during eternity so the more we know about it, the better prepared we will be.

Satisfaction guaranteed, has been the promise of the radio and television advertisements and there seem to be no end to the commercial world's promises to fulfill hopes and dreams. If I may ask; do you know of many truly satisfied people? If you do, can you take me with you just to meet one or two? Because, I would pay anything just to know how long their so-called satisfaction will last. We plan and we save for many years for the perfect vacation and then head off to our dream-come-true exotic destinations.

We indulge in every desire for fun, food and fantasy for a week, two weeks or three weeks or maybe more, and then we head home with wonderful memories of our vacation. It may indeed have been a satisfying one, two, three or more weeks but are we really being fulfilled for the rest of our lives when the vacation is over?

Perhaps you are working hard to build the home and career of your dreams; a place where you are the sole ruler and reign over every affordable luxury and comfort but does it truly satisfy your deepest desires? Just be frank with yourself for a moment; about how long would you say that the pleasures of this world usually last after we have indulged ourselves in them? It was said that an all-time Olympic swimming gold medalist who claimed the highest number of gold medals ever in one Olympic event, plunged into depression few months after such a great victory and accomplishment and as a result started to drink heavily and used abused substances. One would wonder what would cause such a successful athlete to plunge into depression.

This answer is simple. In his book *"Mere Christianity"* C.S. Lewis wrote:

> *"If I find in myself a desire which no experience in this world can satisfy, -the most probable explanation is that I was made for another world, which is heaven, my true home"*.

I selected as the sub-title of this book *The Universal Symphony of Effectual Praise* because the word 'Effectual' according to the Collins English Dictionary – *(Complete & Unabridged 2012 Digital Edition)* means: "being capable of or successful in producing an intended result".

I believe with all my heart and I am of a strong persuasion that our worship should have an intended goal and that achieving this goal should be the primary force propelling every worshipper into the presence of the Most-High God.

The etymology or the word origin of the English word *'effectual'* is from the late Latin word *'effectualis'*, or the Latin *'effectus'* which means accomplishment. This word when used properly has the connotation of actions with a sense of purpose achieving the desired effect aimed at. In simple term, the worshipper should feel a sense of accomplishment or sat-isfaction by the time he or she leaves the pres-ence of the Lord after giving worship, praises and adoration unto the most-high God. After a true worship experience you should feel lighter and feel an incredible sense of relief compared to how you initially entered into God's presence in worship.

> Music is part of worship but good music alone does not constitute worship.

A Universal Symphony because hallelujah, is a universal language that transcends all cultures of the world. It is pronounced almost the same way in every language and tongue across the globe. I have had the privilege to travel to many countries and have enjoyed my association and fellowship with many Pastors, Ministers of the gospel and believers. It's amazing to know that the word hallelujah is pronounced almost the same way in every language I have come across so far.

A true worship experience is therefore that which brings satisfaction and accomplishment to the worshipper. This intended goal, satisfaction or sense of accomplishment, will only be attained if the worshipper has an understanding of what worship is and how to effectually render true worship unto God. One would agree with me that knowledge and understanding is pivotal to the execution of a task in the most effectual way possible.

One can be zealous about worship, but if there is the absence of the necessary knowledge to support his or her zeal, not much would be attained. When I listen to people preach or teach the word of God, and I happen to hear them preach again three to five years later, I always expect more from them than I had previously heard. The reason for this is because our knowledge of God and of the things of God ought to increase in tandem with our walk with God. This is why the Apostle Paul, perhaps out of frustration with the believers in the early church, made a statement to this effect;

> *"For when for the time ye ought to be teachers, ye have need that one teach you again which be the first principles of the oracles of God, and are become such as have need of milk, and not of strong meat."*
> *Hebrews 5:12*

Amongst other goals, one of the major purposes for writing this book is to encourage the believer to praise God in a more effective way than he or she has done in the past. Your understanding and ability to render praise unto God should be better today than it was five or ten years ago.

This book is therefore aimed at proving beyond any reasonable doubt that the mere singing and our congregational responses to 'good music' during our church services does not in itself constitute true worship. True praise and worship should be an experience and not an act or a performance. It should be one that goes far beyond the gratification of the flesh.

True worship ought to be an inner court experience and not just an outer court experience. In other words, music is part of worship but good music in itself does not constitute true worship. In like manner, worship can be noisy, but noise in itself does not necessarily constitute worship. In the days of old, the Israelites carried the ark of the Lord before them into battle and they made so much noise that the earth quaked in the camp of their enemies. In assuming their victory over their enemy was assured, they came to a rude awakening when on the day of battle they were utterly defeated and slain by their enemies, as well as having the ark captured by the Philistines.

In this book, I will explore through an exposition of the first verse of the last chapter of the book of Psalms (Psalms 150:1) four key areas about praise and worship namely;

- What it means to Praise the Lord
- Who ought to Praise the Lord
- How God ought to be Praised
- Where God ought to be Praised

This will culminate with what I have termed in this book as the *Universal Symphony*, where both heaven and earth and all creatures that dwell therein are summoned to usher in praise and worship unto the one and most-high God of all creation.

I therefore invite you to stay on this expository journey with me through the pages and chapters of this book. My promise to you is that by the time you are through with reading this book, your understanding of praise and worship will be completely transformed to higher heights and deeper depths to the glory of God.

Remember that the bible declares that "my people perish for lack of knowledge", hence any opportunity to be enlightened in the word of God and to glean more in addition to what you already know should be one that is welcomed by the people of God.

Chapter One

THE ROLE OF WORSHIP

In the days of old, praise and worship were so central and crucial to the livelihood of God's people that an ultimatum was placed upon the lives of God's people through the scripture to render worship unto the Lord of hosts. This ultimatum according to Zechariah 14:17 could be paraphrased as simply "No worship, no rain":

> *"And it shall be that whoso will not come up of all the families of the earth unto Jerusalem to worship the King, the Lord of hosts, even upon them shall be no rain." (Zechariah 14:17)*

It is worth noting that worship in Jerusalem was pivotal in those days, but, in our day, God is not as particular about the venue as he is about the process. At the time of Jesus, there existed the contention between the Jews and the Samaritans as to which is the right location or venue for worship. Jesus however buried this age-long contention between the Jews and the Samaritans through his discourse with the Samaritan woman at the well. Being a Samaritan, the woman challenged the notion that Jerusalem should be the designated place of worship because the Samaritans held that God should be worshipped in their mountains. Jesus, however, dismissed the venue and placed emphasis on the significance of worship by saying that the time has come and now is that time that true worshippers must worship God in truth and in spirit. This is because *spirit* takes us out of time and space, and *truth* takes us beyond our circumstances.

If only we believers would learn how to praise God more, our battles and burdens will be made much easier and lighter, and our victories would be assured.

> ***"Except the Lord build the house, they labour in vain that build it: except the Lord keep the city, the watchman waketh but in vain. It is vain for you to rise up early, to sit up late, to eat the bread of sorrows: for so he giveth his beloved sleep."***
> ***Psalm 127:1-2***

Contrary to what many of us have been taught growing up, our blessings and prosperity are not contingent upon how hard we work. Instead, our blessings are contingent upon the level of our praise and worship of him, who is the provider of all good things. It is dependent upon the level of our intimacy with God in worship and praise.

"For promotion cometh neither from the east, nor from the west, nor from the south. But God is the judge: he putted down one, and septet up another." Psalm 75:6-7

My question to you is; who is building your house? If it's not the Lord who is building your house, it won't withstand the storms of life and the test of time.

The foundational strength of your spiritual house depends on who the builder is.

We have taught our children to believe that all successes in life come from working hard, so what we instill into their young minds from day to day is to work hard, and harder, and their hardest. You may not agree with me on this, but depending on hard work alone without reliance on God is an ideology that opposes scripture. It is contrary to scripture in every sense as it caters to man's dependency on the arm of flesh. However, the songwriter makes us aware that the arm of flesh will fail; hence we dare not trust in our own strength.

Don't be surprised that I'm saying this because I'm not telling you to be lazy, neither am I telling you not to work. Instead, I'm telling you what to do and that is, instead of exerting so much physical strength, pray harder, worship more, and supplicate more often. Instead of pushing stuff by your own strength, lift them up to God. This is because we spend so much time exerting physical strength, while God actually wants us to do is to learn to worship Him more from the heart. If we become selfless before God, He will open doors for us that no man can close and will shut some doors behind us that no man can open.

I discovered from my studies of the bible that when God finds someone who is over qualified for a task, He first strips them of their qualifications before equipping them for the task that He has called them to do. There are numerous accounts in the bible where God had to literally strip men and women of their achievements so He could work through them in order to accomplish His divine will and purpose.

As an example, when God found Moses, God said to him, you are over qualified for the task of leading my people out of bondage. You have been trained in the royal palaces of Pharaoh. You have been trained in the

Egyptian way and mindset, and groomed as heir to the throne of Egypt. Hence God's proposal to Moses when he attempted to use his acquired skills to the rescue of an Israelite from the perils of his Egyptian task master was that: "I can't use you as you are now", rather, God would have Moses to go to the land of Midian as a run-away convict escaping from the hands of justice.

It was while in Midian that God trained Moses to learn patience by tending to the flock of his father-in-law Jethro. The training was so intense and effective that by the time God was through with Moses, the man who was once described in the book of Acts as being great in word when he left Egypt, later described himself as one who lack the ability to speak well.

In the fullness of time when God was through with Moses after 40 years of training in the hot scorching desert of Midian; God then sent him back to the same place that he was running away from. His new assignment was to deliver his people the Israelites from their bondage in Egypt not by the application of the Egyptian wisdom acquire in the palace of Pharaoh, but rather by the wisdom of God acquired in the desolate desert of Midian. .

As another example, God did something similar with the life of the Apostle Paul after his conversion experience on the road of Damascus. Paul (then Saul) was as educated as Moses. Similarly, God was saying to Paul at the point of his conversion as he had said to Moses; "you are too smart for your own good, and as a Pharisee, you are too righteous for your own good".

So like Moses, God had to send Paul to Arabia, and whilst there, God had to strip him of all his prior qualifications in order to prepare him for the great task he had for him; as one of the main authors of the New Testament.

From time to time God does the same to todays' believer just so we will not be tempted to attribute our victories to our own accomplishments in the flesh. This is because by the time God is through with us, we would have learnt not to attribute our successes to our own doings but rather learn to give all the glory to God, to whom it truly belongs. Remember that God has said in His word that His glory will He not share with any man.

I'm by no means discouraging you from pursuing your ambitions and aspirations in life because I believe in working hard as well. However, when you come to God, please don't allow the worldly accomplishments like your degrees earned; awards achieved, or recognitions bestowed upon you be the things that you rely on in order to fulfill your God given mandate or calling in the Lord. In Philippians 3;4-9, we read about the seven bragging rights of the Apostle Paul in accordance with his personal achievements, as shown in the text below;

⁴ though I also might have confidence in the flesh. If anyone else thinks he may have confidence in the flesh, I more so:

**⁵ circumcised the eighth day,
Of the stock of Israel,
Of the tribe of Benjamin,
A Hebrew of the Hebrews;
Concerning the law, a Pharisee;
⁶ Concerning zeal, persecuting the church;
concerning the righteousness which is in the law, blameless
.⁷ But what things were gain to me, these I have counted loss for Christ.
⁸ Yet indeed I also count all things loss for the excellence of the knowledge of Christ Jesus my Lord, for whom I have suffered the loss of all things, and count them as rubbish, that I may gain Christ ⁹ and be found in Him, not having my own righteousness, which is from the law, but that which is through faith in Christ, the righteousness which is from God by faith; Philippians 3;4-9**

In conclusion Paul counted all his accolades as dung or garbage, just so he will gain Christ. That is the point I want to make because at the end of our earthly journey, it is only what is done for Christ that will last. I pray you don't get me wrong because I'm not saying all your education and hard work is of no value; neither am I saying that it's not worth having personal accomplishments. What I'm implying is that you don't have to do all that in order for God to bless you or use you. God wants you to simply praise him. He wants you to pray and to supplicate. He wants you to fast and to seek his face with sincerity of heart: "*......And all these things shall then be added unto you*". The flip side of this is that, when God finds someone that is not qualified enough, He builds them and brings them up to the place of readiness so they can accomplish His will. A perfect example of this is a shepherd boy in the bible named David. When God found His servant David, he was not qualified, he was not a warrior like his predecessor King Saul, and he was not as gigantic or perhaps as good-looking as King Saul. As a matter of fact, he was working outside in the field, keeping the flock of his father Jesse while his older siblings were engaged in Israel's battle with the Philistines. David was not aware of the palace protocol. He had not been trained in the use of armory like Saul. His father was a shepherd therefore he is without pedigree; but God saw in David raw material that could be used for his glory. David's raw material was his love for worship and his ability to worship God under any circumstances.

After God's disappointment with King Saul, God finally finds somebody who is genuinely seeking after him. God knew that irrespective of failures and downfalls, David was going to worship him and remain a true worshipper until the point of his death. While many drifted away from God and were never able to make their way back into the merciful arms of the Almighty, David always pressed his way back to God no matter how far he drifted away. That is why he was able to write; ***"As the deer panteth after the water brooks, so panteth my soul after thee O'Lord".*** Do you have a heart that pants after God, that will find its way back to God no matter how far off you happen to drift away?

During a recent veteran's day celebration, America's oldest veteran alive who is 108 years, was interviewed by the news media and asked about his secret for living that long; to my uttermost surprise, and disappointment, he attributed the cause for the long length of his days to drinking whisky. In response to this, I said to myself that the devil is a liar because, how can one attribute the reason for the long length of his days to drinking whisky instead of giving glory to the Almighty God who has kept him through the rough and rugged terrains of a long life on earth?

Some folks in like manner, have attributed their successes in life to the caliber of school they attended or to the line of profession they pursued. Instead of giving God the glory that is due His name they have redirected the glory to their alma mater or career paths.

Your success as a believer in Jesus Christ has nothing to do with whether or not you went to Harvard, Yale, Columbia or Cornell just to name a few of the Ivy League Colleges. I want to call to your memory of the fact that; had it not been for the Lord who was on your side, you would have ended up on the street corners, in the pot houses or in the homeless shelters across this city just like those you see in these places. You are no better than the people you see in these places except for the fact that God has been good to you and by His mercies, He has shown His favor upon your life. Quit directing the glory to the wrong sources and redirect it unto God from whom all blessing flow.

Chapter Two

A MAN AFTER GOD'S OWN HEART

I n I Samuel 13:14 we find these words about David *"But now thy kingdom shall not continue: the Lord hath sought him a man after his own heart, and the Lord hath commanded him to be captain over his people, because thou hast not kept that which the Lord commanded thee."* This psalm was probably written by David while he was on the run away from his son Absalom, at the verge of what may have led to a disintegration of his Kingdom. David at this point in his life, compared his thirst for God to that of a deer in search for water to quench its thirst. This is no doubt the cry of a desperate soul in search for answers to the twists and turns of life. It's upon this note that David wrote in the book of Psalm ";*As the deer panteth after the water brooks, so panteth my soul after thee, O God. [2] My soul thirsteth for God, for the living God: when shall I come and appear before God? [3] My tears have been my meat day and night, while they continually say unto me, Where is thy God? [4] When I remember these things, I pour out my soul in me: for I had gone with the multitude, I went with them to the house of God, with the voice of joy and praise, with a multitude that kept holyday. [5] Why art thou cast down, O my soul? and why art thou disquieted in me? hope thou in God: for I shall yet praise him for the help of his countenance. [6] O my God, my soul is cast down within me: therefore will I remember thee from the land of Jordan, and of the Hermonites, from the hill Mizar. [7] Deep calleth unto deep at the noise of thy waterspouts: all thy waves and thy billows are gone over me. Psalm 42:1-7*

The phrase "deep calleth unto deep" has its roots from the story of creation in the book of Genesis.

And God said, Let there be a firmament in the midst of the waters, and let it divide the waters from the waters. [7] And God made the firmament, and divided the waters which were under the firmament from the waters which were above the firmament: and it was so. [8] And God

called the firmament Heaven. And the evening and the morning were the second day. Genesis 1:6-9

[9] And God said, Let the waters under the heaven be gathered together unto one place, and let the dry land appear: and it was so.

The object of David's affection is to be in worship before God's presence.

So every now and then, the waters above the firmament, yearns to communicate with the *waters* below the firmament.

The deep above cries out unto the deep beneath. This might be what David alluded to when he wrote;

7] Deep calleth unto deep at the noise of thy waterspouts: all thy waves and thy billows are gone over me.

God described David as a man after His heart. If one doesn't examine carefully the point of view from which God was speaking, one may think that God was positioning David to the status of a man he has chosen to be after his heart. But that is not the interpretation of this scripture. It's important to note that the meaning of this scripture is contingent upon where one places the word *after*.

If the word '*after*' is use to describe God's attitude towards David, it brings out an entirely different meaning from when the word *after* is used to describe David's desperation for God. I believe with all conviction that it's the later that applies in this case because it's David who is always in the face of God. Whether happy or sad, whether David feels accomplished or needs comfort. Whether in the will of God or in need of forgiveness, he was always in the face of God. Notice that although David kills Goliath, however his heart was never after Goliath.

He conquered great nations, but his heart was never after these nations. He was blessed with riches, silver and gold, but his heart was never after wealth. He had fame, but his heart never craved for fame. As a matter of fact, David was ready to relinquish his crown and kingdom in order to gain God's approval, favor, acceptance and God's presence.

That is why in response to God's anger against him in Psalm 51;11 David pleaded with God to take all he wished to take away from him except for God's holy presence. It was David who wrote; **"Cast me not away from thy presence, and take not thy Holy Spirit away from me."**

God was the only one who consumed David's focus. There was only one object of his affection and that's why he was able to utter such words as; *"My soul thirsteth for*

God, for the living God: when shall I come and appear before God"

God was of course not putting David on any pedestal by declaring that David is a man after his own heart. God was not putting David anywhere that David would personally not want to be. On the contrary, it was David who was pursuing after the heart of God. It was David who was chasing after the presence of God. It was David who was always lifting up holy hands in worship before God, whether in the heart of the scourging and desolate desert with his flock or in the comfort of his palace. No matter where he was or where he found himself, his heart was always pursuing after God.

When a man finds himself in love with a woman and is pursuing after the heart of the woman, he does everything he can and apply every skill in order to make the best impression and win the heart of his newly found lover.

He doesn't give up and is not deterred until he is able to win the heart of the woman he loves.

In my opinion, the greatest accolade God could ever bestow upon any mortal is to be called "A man after God's own Heart"

So was David "he was after the heart of God so much that nothing could deter him from following after God. In other words, he was always in the face of God such that it was like everywhere God turned, there comes David seeking after him. When David was happy, he was in the presence of God. When David was sad, he was in the presence of God. When David was threatened by his enemies, he was in the presence of God. When David sinned against God, he was in the presence of God. When David finds himself in any mess, he was in the presence of God. When David has a bad day, he was in the presence of God. He was always "in the face of God" which is why God said "this man is after my heart". In other words, God is not putting David in a position that he may not want to be. On the contrary, it's David who was constantly pursuing after God's heart and wanted more of God. Do you really want more of God? Then, why are you not pursuing him as seriously as David did? The song writer said *"All day long, I have been with Jesus, All day long, my heart has uttered praise, All day long my heart, my soul keeps searching, for whom my soul love"*.

God called Abraham his friend, He called Moses the meekest, and John the Baptist the greatest born of a woman but God' description of David as 'a man after his own heart' in my opinion, is the greatest accolade that God would ever bestow upon any mortal being. It is said of the deer that when it is thirsty, it will run for days and would not stop until it finally finds ditches of water to quench its thirst.

Notice that unlike David, King Saul never cared too much about God's presence. According to Chronicles 13:3, **"they sought not after the ark in the days of Saul"** but with David the presence of God was all that mattered to him. That's why God will always place a demarcation between the worshipper and the non-worshipper.

A COMPARISON BETWEEN KING DAVID AND KING SAUL

(1) Saul was more a warrior and a giant, when he was called of God.
  David was just a little Shepherd boy.
(2) Saul was anointed with a vial (flask) of oil which signifies fragility.
  David on the other hand, was anointed with a horn which is a symbol of the longevity of his kingdom.
(3) Saul was anointed once.
  David was anointed three times and after the third anointing, he took down the stronghold of Zion.
(4) Saul did not care so much about the presence of God. For I Chronicles. 13:3 reads; *"for we inquire not at the ark in the days of Saul"*,

On the contrary, the presence of God meant everything to David. According I Sam. 28:6, the first thing he sought to do when he ascended to the throne of Israel as king, was

to recover the Ark of the Covenant which sig-
nify God's presence.

So much was David's passion for God that
in Psalm 51, when he sinned against God by
sleeping with Bathsheba the wife if Uriah, he
was willing to let go of all his kingdom and
possessions except for God's presence. That's
the reason why he cried out unto God with
these desperate words;

**"Create in me a clean heart O' Lord,
and renew a right Spirit within me.
Cast me not away from thy presence
Lord. Take not thy Holy Spirit from
me. Restore unto me, the joy of thy
salvation."**

The Samaritan woman's attempt to
draw water from the well was to fulfill
a need. Except that she had so many
needs in her life and did not know
which one to start with.

And so God said to Saul "you refused to
worship" and to David he said "you consis-
tently worshiped me" therefore this indi-
cates that God will always place a distinction
between the non-worshipper and the true
worshipper. We cannot afford to worship once
in a week and then wait till another Sunday
comes around before approaching the throne
of grace with our worship. We must take our
worship beyond the Sunday morning and

evening services. When you wake up in the morning, I challenge you to lift up your voice in worship unto the Lord. When you put that car keys in the ignition, I challenge you to begin to lift up your voice unto God with a sacrifice of praise and worship. When you are retiring to your bed after the toil of the day, I challenge you to lift up you voice and say; *"I will bless the Lord at all times and His praise shall continually be in my mouth"*.

The Samaritan woman that Jesus met at the well was like David in a sense because she was drawing water. She was trying to fulfill a need in her life but she just didn't know which one because she had so many needs. Although she had a need for relationship, she also had a spiritual thirst inside her that she didn't even understand. Jesus said to her, the hour cometh and now is hour that the Father is searching for true worshippers; for they that worship God must worship him in spirit and in truth.

Spirit; takes you out of time and space, while *truth*, takes you out of your circumstances. That's why the bible says the ye shall know the truth and the truth you know shall sets you free. This means that your worship is not contingent upon your circumstances or the condition in which you find yourself; whether things are good or bad: we ought to bless the Lord at all times. The devil can try you intensely but he can't take your worship. Your spouse may walk away from you, but your worship is not dependent on his or her presence; your worship is in God. God forbid; but you may even be ill on your sick bed but that shouldn't impede your worship. People may not even treat you well but it doesn't matter whether people treat you good or not; God has always been good to you and he deserves your worship.

When you come into the presence of the Lord, forget about those people and whether or not they treat you good or bad and just give God the praise that He alone deserves. Because if it had not been for the Lord who was on your side, the enemy would have devoured you as a prey.

Our soul is escaped as a bird out of the snares of the fowler; the snares are broken and we are escaped. Our help is in the name of the Lord who made heaven and earth. Psalm 124:7

Your faith and dependence on God has to be so strong that neither hell nor high-waters would be able to separate you from the love of God that is in Christ Jesus. That's what makes David distinct from Saul, because he allowed no circumstance to impede his worship of God.

It's David that wrote those many beautiful psalms of praise and worship because he knew how to be persistent in his worship unto God.

I discovered that you can talk about a worshipper all you want but you just can't slow down or stop their worship.

God open doors for worshippers and puts them in places and in positions where they don't deserve simply because they praise him. They may not have the required education or experience but because they praise him, God elevates them to sit in high places. He honors them just because they praise Him.

When every day is a battle and when things are thrown at you from every side, it's an indication that you are closer to your breakthrough so don't let unfavorable circumstances steal your worship. If the Patriarch Jacob was here, he would bear witness of what I'm talking about when he had to wrestle with an angel of the Lord until day break.

Normally it's when you are close to your breakthrough that you feel like fainting. The symptoms of fainting do not come at the start of a journey and neither does it come in the middle. It's towards the eleventh hour or the midnight hour, when it seems like all hell is breaking loose on you. That's when you are close to your victory and the reason why you feel that way is because your daylight is about to break forth. Although weeping may endure for the night be assured that joy cometh in the morning. Hold on in praise and worship unto God because your morning is closer than you ever think and you are about to break forth into singing any moment from now if you don't quit.

> **Sing, O barren, thou that didst not bear; break forth into singing, and cry aloud, thou that didst not travail with child: for more are the children of the desolate than the children of the married wife, saith the Lord [2] Enlarge the place of thy tent, and let them stretch forth the curtains of thine habitations: spare not, lengthen thy cords, and strengthen thy stakes;[3] For thou shalt break forth on the right hand and on the left; and thy seed shall inherit the Gentiles, and make the desolate cities to be inhabited. Isaiah 54:1-3**

Don't allow even church folks to stop your praise; let them know that you were born to praise God; you were designed to praise God; you came out from your mother's womb purposely to praise God and that you will go to your grave praising God; because your praise is not between you and them; your praise is between you and your God.

Some people have testimonies that could result in them running around and praising God in the loudest voice in church but the problem is that they are too intimidated by the faces of people. These people however, don't know your sorrows and are not acquainted with your grief or pain; so how dare they judge your worship? It's not between you and them; it's between you and your God, so whenever you find yourself in the presence of God just ignore those who don't like or appreciate your worship and give unto God the praise that He deserves for His goodness towards you.

And so I want you to know that where the Spirit of the Lord is; there is liberty so don't ignore that liberty but rather make the best use of it in God's presence. Let the earth rejoice and be glad at the sound of the trumpet and at the voices of true worshippers; For the Lord is good and His mercies endure forever.

Chapter Three

THE DIFFERENT FORMS
OF WORSHIP

*Praise ye the Lord. Praise God in his sanctuary: Praise him in the firmament of his power. [2] Praise him for his mighty acts: praise him according to his excellent greatness. [3] Praise him with the sound of the trumpet: praise him with the psaltery and harp. [4] Praise him with the timbrel and dance: praise him with stringed instruments and organs. [5] Praise him upon the loud cymbals: praise him upon the high sounding cymbals. [6] Let everything that hath breath praise the Lord. **Praise ye the Lord**. Psalm 150:1-6*

I found out through my studies that in the Hebrew, there are at least six or more different words translated as praise in English. Each of these words depicts or demonstrates the various ways in which God ought to be praised and worshipped.

It's worth noting that none of these six or more ways is found to be complete in itself; and perhaps that explains the reason why there are six or perhaps even more ways in the first place. In this chapter, I will give a brief description of five Hebrew words translated as 'praise' in English and I will identify as well as examine the major characteristics of each of these words, while expounding on how each of these forms of praise ought to be executed in liturgical worship. Additionally, I will expound in more detail the sixth and last major form of praise in the next chapter. The sixth form of praise will form the key to understanding what it literally means to praise the Lord.

1) SHABACH

The praise word *Shabach*, means to praise with a loud voice. It means to cry out unto the Lord. It carries the notion of addressing someone in a loud tone. Other synonyms of Shabach are to; commend glory, keep in praise, still, triumph. In its simplest terms, it also means to congratulate.

2) TODAH

This second word for Praise means; to praise in the form of giving thanks unto the Lord. It has to do with the offering of thanks, whether through songs, poetry or the giving of your substance etc.

In *Ezra 10:11*, Todah is expressed both as praise rendered by acknowledging and abandoning sin. It is also thanksgiving in songs of liturgical worship as done by a choir or congregation as a whole.

It's properly rooted in the extension of the hand, i.e. (by implication) avowal, or (usually) adoration; specifically, a choir of worshippers–confession, sacrifice of praise, thanksgiving and offering.

3) TEHILLAH

The Hebrew praise word *Tehillah* is the act of general or public praise as described especially *Psalm 22:4; Psalm 33:1; Psalm 106:12; Nehemiah 12:46.* Psalm 100:4 describes entering his gates with thanksgiving, and into his courts with praise.

The Meaning of Tehillah is rooted in the rendering of songs of praise unto the Lord in expression of His greatness, goodness and mercies. One would notice that in the Psalms, one often come across the phrase "I will sing a new song unto the Lord"; this is unrehearsed expressions of praise that burst out from within whether in songs any other form of expression of gratitude. This constitute an expression of praise in the form of Tehillah.

4) ZAMAR

This praise word means to make music in praise of God and to praise God on the instruments of music. In Psalms 150 the worshipper is commanded to; "Praise him on the harp, praise Him with the cymbal, praise Him with the string instruments and organ" etc. To adore God on the pipe, play on a reed; As in *Psalm 147:1* to make music or melody. *Psalm 108:2* as an instrumental accompaniment. Zamar as a form of praise is rooted in the playing of musical instruments.

A primitive root of the word, carries the idea of striking with the fingers; or more properly, to touch the strings or parts of a musical instrument, i.e. to play skillfully upon it; to make music, accompanied by the voice; hence to celebrate in song and music. To give praise, sing forth praises as well as Psalms unto God.

5) YADAH

The origin of yadah (pronounced as *yaw-daw*) is quite interesting. By definition, Yadah means to throw or cast something in the direction that you want it to go. Hence our praises must be directional. Meaning, it must have an intended destination and that destination must be to the one who supplies our needs according to His riches and glory in Christ Jesus. Some people direct their praises unto chariots and horses but we have an obligation to direct our praises unto the one and only wise God. God therefore must be the sole destination of our praise.

Coming from an idolatrous background, I am very careful to whom I direct my praise to. Born into a royal lineage in Africa, my family has deep roots in idol worship. My grand-father was the chief of our district and my father was in line to be the crowned prince, which would eventually lead me to being heir to the idolatrous throne of my fathers but I'm thankful to God for his mighty hand of salvation that redirected my life into ministering unto Him, instead of ministering unto Satan.

So what Yadah really means is to throw up praise unto God. It also means to confess or to acknowledge. It's derived, perhaps from gestures accompanying the act of; giving thanks, laud, and praise; cast out, make confession, praise, shoot, expression of thankfulness or gratitude.

A literal translation would be to use (i.e. Hold out) the hand; physically, to throw (a stone, an arrow) at or away; especially to revere or worship with extended hands. Intensively, to bemoan by wringing the hands or to cast out, make confess or to shoot, and give thanks or simply be thankful.

So notice when David goes to fight Goliath; that he did not exert any great physical strength. This symbolized worship in the form of yadah. He simply finds a rock, which scripturally signifies Christ because the book of Hebrew makes us to understand that the rock is a typology of the person of Jesus Christ. This symbolizes worship in the form of yadah. David then launched the rock in a direction, which signifies the praise word; yadah.

This is because as noted earlier, yadah means to put something in your hand and thrust it in the direction in which you target it to go. So when Goliath came against David, David said to King Saul, "I can't go with your heavy armory Saul, I have got something that You don't know about; something that I have been cultivating all these years as a shepherd boy alone on the fields with my father's flock which is called worship and I'm getting ready to give God some praise"

Besides, David had not proven what King Saul was putting on him and therefore had no confidence in it. Rather, David relied on the kind of weapon that he had proven which is called praise and worship. It was in praise and worship of his God that he had confidence in because he had proven it against the lion and the bear which attempted to devour his father's flock while he was shepherding the flock away from home. That's the trusted weapon that he eventually used against the uncircumcised Philistine.

The experience of David as a worshipper compared to King Saul places Saul as one who did not care much about the things of God. Again, this leads me to say that God will always set a demarcation between the worshipper and the non-worshipper. David had a heart that was always desperate for more of God. No doubt his soul was always desperate for a worship experience in the presence of God.

Chapter Four

PRAISE YE THE LORD
Psalm 150:1a

HALAL

The sixth and last Hebrew word for praise that I would like to discuss in this book is the word *halal*. To expound on the meaning of this word, I would like to draw your attention to the first phrase of Psalm 150:1

> ***"Praise ye the Lord.** Praise God in his sanctuary: praise him in the firmament of his power. "*

There is a group of Psalms in the bible that are known as the *halallic* Psalms. This name is derived from the word *halal* which is one of the Hebrew words translated as praise in English.

You would notice when you carefully compare the last five chapters of the book of Psalms (from Psalms 146 to Psalm 150) that all these Psalms *(Ps. 146; 147; 148; 149 & 150)* begin with the phrase **"Praise ye the Lord"** as well as to end with the phrase **"Praise ye the Lord".** Consequently, this makes the halallic Psalms very easy to be identified.

These Psalms are evidently meant for liturgical use as a format for public worship. According to bible scholars, the halallic Psalms are the Psalms that the Jews sang at the Feast of the First Fruits after the nation Israel had harvested their crops and celebrated the increase that God had brought to them at the end of a farming season.

It is also worth noting that the Old Testament was written in the Hebrew language and the phrase "Praise ye the Lord" as seen in Psalms 150:1, is represented by just one Hebrew word and that word is; Hallelujah.

Therefore, the Jewish Masoretic text reads this way; instead of the phrase 'praise ye the Lord' as found in our English bibles, it begins with the word Hallelujah and ends with Hallelujah. Meaning that the four-worded phrase *'Praise ye the Lord'* as found in the English is translated as only one Hebrew word Hallelujah.

(See below for how Psalm 150 reads in the Jewish Tanakh)

1. ***Hallelujah,*** Praise God in His sanctuary; Praise Him in the firmament of His power.

2 Praise Him for His mighty acts; Praise Him according to His abundant greatness.

3. Praise Him with the blast of the horn; Praise Him with the psaltery and harp.

4. Praise Him with the timbrel and dance; Praise Him with stringed instruments and the pipe.

5. Praise Him with the loud-sounding cymbals; Praise Him with the clanging cymbals.

6. Let everything that hath breath praise the LORD. ***Hallelujah.***

*(Psalm 150- Taken From JPS Tanakh 1917)
TAKEN FROM THE HOLY SCRIPTURES; ***ACCORDING TO THE MASORETIC TEXT–Jewish Publication Society***

"Hallelujah"–is an imperative, meaning it is a command. It's therefore an unavoidable obligation that demands attention or action.

Notice that in Psalms 150, although it's a short Psalm comprising of only six verses, the word 'praise' (Halal in the Hebrew) occurs 13 times in that chapter alone.

Notice also that the word "Hallelujah" is an imperative, meaning it is an unavoidable obligation or requirement that demands attention or action. This therefore makes it a command. Due to lack of proper understanding in today's church, when one says Hallelujah, the usual response has been to repeat back the word Hallelujah. This is however an incorrect response since the word Hallelujah by interpretation is commanding us to praise the Lord. As we all know, commands by their nature are not meant to be repeated but rather to be implemented or acted upon.

Therefore the right response when one says Hallelujah; ought to be putting into action, what the command instructs you to do, which is to praise the Lord in every possible way and with every possible word or expression you know that can be used in praising God.

The transliteration or the literal translation for, "Praise ye the Lord" in the Hebrew goes like this; "Ye praise the Lord". The reason 'ye' has to be placed first is because Hallelujah is an imperative and hence a command and therefore it ought to begin with a pronoun. That pronoun happen to be the old Elizabethan English word 'Ye'. Modern English frequently confuses the two common pronouns *ye* and *thou* as found in King James English version of the bible.

Thou = refers to *one person*
Ye = means *'you', or 'all of you'*

This means that ones' response to Hallelujah is an obligation and hence the response to hallelujah is not negotiable. This also means that whether you want to or not, you are obligated to praise God in response to the command "Praise ye the Lord".

You have to understand that this is not the English of Shakespeare. This is what is known as 'Elizabethan English' (the English spoken in the Elizabethan era in England and the United Kingdom). The Elizabethan English has the following structure;

1st person	*singular*	I
	plural	we
2nd person	*singular*	thou
	plural	ye, you
3rd person	*singular*	he/she/it
	plural	they

It therefore means that whether you are rich or poor, regardless of whether you are educated or uneducated, whether you are Black or White or Hispanic or Indian or of whatever ethnic origin or decent, Hallelujah is a command that is all inclusive.

Remember that the Hebrew word for Praise is halal therefore "ye praise the Lord" is a command for you to halal Yah (Hallelujah). Since Hallelujah is made up of the two Hebrew words namely *halal* and *Yah*, I would therefore like to expound on the meaning of these two Hebrew words one after the other.

1) Halal

What exactly does Halal mean in the Hebrew? The meaning of the word 'praise' is fuzzy in the English but the Hebrew language gives us a very clear and concise meaning to the word *halal*, which is translated as praise in the English.

Below are examples of what the word *halal* means in the Hebrew.

It means:

1) To make clear
2) To make something shine
3) To show off
4) To rave or freak out
5) To make a boast, to celebrate or to go wild about something
6) To act insanely or to be driven madly
7) It means to be a fanatic (from which we get the word 'fans'- like the Yankee fans or Met fans)
*8) It also means to be clamorously foolish and to make a fool of yourself in public.

In my research on the meanings of halal, the expression that strikes me most is the fact that halal also means to make a 'spectacle' out of yourself in public. In other words, to halal God literally mean to behave in such a way that you could be easily noticed, or in a way that you cannot be missed even among a crowd of people. This therefore means that praising the Lord or to *halal* God in the purest and finest meaning of the word, should look much more different than we see in our churches today. This also means that there is nothing gentle or polished about praising the Lord.

Halal, literally means to make a spectacle of yourself in such a way that you cannot be missed in a crowd of people.

When the Yankees or the Mets are playing against any opposing teams, they always have their fans alongside with them that will go any distance to cheer their team whether their team is winning or losing. The reason for this is because they are fanatics (fans) of the teams they support.

At times one would see on television that these Yankee or Mets fanatics would paint their faces blue and red, jump and scream at the top of their voices just to cheer their team and show how proud they are of their respective teams. In like manner to halal Yah (God Almighty), means to be a 'Yah fanatic'. Hence, if some Knicks or Nets fans will go all that distance to madly cheer their team on, simply because some sport man shoots a leather ball into a metal hoop, although they reap no personal benefits from their support of these teams, how much more ought we, the Yah fanatics behave in worship to God who gives us life and breath. We ought to praise God, who is the essence of our existence and the creator and giver of our lives in an even much greater way than these sporting fans will do. If I consider the length and breathe that these fans will go in support of their team, then how much more ought we to shout and praises our God from the top of our voices, run about, raise our hands and display before Him like David did when he danced before the Lord on the occasion of the return of the Ark of the Covenant to Jerusalem.

> Praising God the bibliocentric way is in strange contrast to modern day notions of sobriety in worship.

Frankly speaking, we owe God a million or trillion times more of our praises, thanks-giving and adoration than what the Mets or Yankee fans render to their sporting clubs. Hasn't God been good enough to you, to deserve a scream, or shout or dance when you come before his presence in worship and adoration?

Notice that although the first missionaries of the gospel were from Europe, this act of worship described as 'halal' is not from a Euro-centric origin. This is because the first Jews were not Europeans by descent. They were olive looking people, most of them being dark skin people from the continent of Africa. The reason why you will not see the word 'Africa' in the bible is because that was not the orig-inal name of the continent in bible days. The continent Africa was named after a Roman General however the name of the continent many years before it become known as Africa, was Ethiopia. The word Ethiopia occurs in many translations of the Old Testament, but it's principally referred to as Kush or the land of Cush. Ethiopia is the land of burnt skin people and when something is burnt, we all know that it's obviously no other color than black.

Therefore this type of worship unknown as *halal*, is from an Ethiopic and Asiatic origin. It's not Eurocentric, because although our modern day liturgy has a great degree of European influence, it is worth noting that the church did not begin from Europe. This bibliocentric form of worship known as halal therefore has its roots from an Ethiopic, Asiatic origin. So, praising God the bibliocentric way is in strange contrast to modern day notions of sobriety in worship, where people come to church in their 'blessed quietness' and sit still in the pews of our churches like Egyptian mummies while the awesome presence and power of God is moving among His congregation.

This backdrop of the origin of worship therefore leads me to my next point. That is, to understand Psalm 150 more precisely, it's worth looking into the life of the one who wrote most if not the entire psalm; David the son of Jesse, the shepherd boy whom God made a king. God made him King because he understood and knew how to worship God.

David obviously, understood what it means to *Halal-Yah* because, even as King, he was ready to loose himself of the dignity that comes with such a highly esteemed position as a king and to literally display before God in unadulterated worship. It was David that wrote those beautiful words of the psalms such as "I will enter into his gates with thanksgiving and into his courts with praise". It was David who said; "I will bless the Lord at all times and his praise shall continually be in my mouth." It was David that danced before the Lord while the ark was on its way from the household of Obed-Edom into the city of Jerusalem. It was David that made a spectacle of himself by dancing before the Lord until his clothes fell off from him. Notice that although his wife, Micah (the daughter of Saul) felt ashamed about David's display of gratitude in worship, however that did not stop David from rendering unto God, the praise that is due his name, because no one can stop a true worshipper from praising his or her God.

God will always stand in defense of the true worshipper. Notice that it was God, and not David who took issue with the comments made by Micah. It was God and not David who got offended by Micah's mockery of David. It was God not David, who reacted to the mockery by shutting the womb of Micah so she could not be able to bear children. That goes to say that when you have an issue with the way people worship God, you have taken on an issue with God. We therefore ought to be very careful not to criticize people simply because we are unwilling to express ourselves in worship to God in the manner in which others will do. Perhaps we lack the boldness to do so, or we feel too dignified to express ourselves before God in public worship service.

What you may not perhaps understand is that, for some people, worshipping God the way they do; by dancing, jumping, skipping, and summersaults or with a loud voice and screaming, is their only way of keeping sane. In other words, their screams, dances and shouts are their only means of venting off the stress and tensions off from their lives. For others, freaking out and raving in God's presence in worship in a manner that may seem insane to you, is just their way to stay alive and not die from the hustles and bustles of this life. Honestly speaking, before I did the research towards the writing of this book on praise and worship, I did not understand why some would worship God the way they do but now, I know and understand why.

2) Yah
Who is *Yah*?. Since the Jews and the Scribes refuse to write out the name of God in

full because God's name is Holy, they instead abbreviated the name of God as simply *Yah.*

'Yah'–Is the present tense of the verb *"To be"*. So therefore, a good translation of the verb "To be" in the present tense will be "I am**".**

Jehovah, refers to the one bringing
into being, the life-giver; the
giver of existence, creator;
he who brings to pass.

No wonder in the burning bush experience when Moses ask God for his name, God simply told him to say to Pharaoh that, "I am" have sent thee.

'I am' means the self-existing one. This in turn means that He is the central source from which all other sources emanated. The philosophers refer to him as "the immovable mover". God is the one who make promises and keep his promises from generations to generations. *Yah*; is the covenant-keeping God. *Yah* is the one who makes contracts and faithfully fulfill His end of the contract. He is the All-Sufficient God and the ancient of days. *Yah* is the one who has no beginning nor ending. He never began and he will never seize to exist. He is the Alpha and the Omega (first letter of the Greek alphabetic as well as the last letter thereof) because He has no beginning of days.

Praising God the biblio-centric way,
is not the same as the "blessed

quietness" that is seen in our
churches from time to time.

According to Strong's Concordance the proper name of the God of Israel is *Jehovah* and it's spelt without vowels, (Yhvh). Pronounced as: *(yeh-ho-vaw),* Jehovah, refers to the one bringing into being, the life-giver; the giver of existence, creator; he who brings to pass, the performer of his promises. He who causes to fall, rain or lightning; the one who is: *i.e.* the absolute and unchangeable one, the existing, ever living, as self-consistent and unchangeable, the one ever coming into manifestation as the God of redemption, he will be it, i.e. all that His servants look for.

Jehovah is not used in Genesis, but is given in *Exodus 3:12-15* as the name of the God who revealed Himself to Moses at Horeb, and is explained thus: I shall be with thee (Exodus 3:12), which is then implied in; I shall be the one who will be. (Exodus 3:14)

Other interpretations are: **I am he who I am,** i.e. that means it is no concern of yours. I am who I am, he who is essentially unnamable, inexplicable.

In the Elohistic group of *Psalm 42-83* (the Elohim Psalms) it is used 39 times. According to Strong's Exhaustive Concordance, Jehovah the Lord from *hayah;* the self-Existent or Eternal; Jehovah, the Jewish national name of God.

That is why when coming into His presence, one must enter into his gates with thanksgiving and into His courts with praise. Notice that thanksgiving, according to the Psalmist, can only bring you through the gates because thanksgiving only expresses our gratitude for the things He has done. Praise and worship on the other hand, is rendered unto God not based on what He has done for us but rather, it is based on who He is regardless of what He has or has not done. Hence, in order to proceed beyond His gates, and into His courts, one would need to *Halal* (praise) Him. Praising God therefore is not the same as the "blessed quietness" that we see in our churches from time to time.

Halal means to make a boast or to rave before *Yah* and if you want to know what it means to Halal or to Praise God, or what the true way of worship should look like; it would be similar to the way football or basketball fans cheer for their teams on the court or in the stadium.

Whenever you get the opportunity to come into His Sanctuary, you ought to make your visit worthwhile, because you don't praise God only when things are good; you also ought to *Halal* God, when things are not going well because in the process, you want to get His undivided attention.

In the Yankee stadium the Yankee fanatics *Halal* their team, but in the Sanctuary of our God, we the *Yah* fanatics Halal our Redeemer.

When people with doctoral degrees and public dignitaries attend the ball game, they scream, jump and shout in support of their team so why is it that they withhold themselves from doing the same when they are invited into the presence of the one who gave them breathe. If some athlete throwing a ball through a hoop will make the Knicks fans scream and jump how much more should we believers display before the God who gives us life and breath.

Praising God should be like being in a crowd of people or in the open public place with the intent to attract the attention of everyone that passes by. In order to achieve this goal, one cannot stand still in some corner with hands folded or hands in pocket. In order to make a spectacle of yourself in public, you ought to be screaming, shouting or acting in a manner that would attract peoples' attention to you, and that is how we ought to praise the Lord when we come into His presence. We ought to praise Him with the raising of hands, jumping on the feet, bowing of the knees, shouting out His name and making a spectacle of ourselves before His presence. Therefore, for those who get offended when people are screaming, and running around in church during worship, please don't be any longer because they are simply expressing themselves in the form of a '*Halal* praise.

Like blind Bartimaeus, the idea behind shouting God's name is that; if you are calling on the Lord and making all that spectacle of yourself, you will definitely not be missed in His presence. No wonder Jesus did not miss blind Bartimaeus. It is because he was the kind of person who would simply not shut up in the face of opposition. He would not take 'no' for an answer until he eventually caught the attention of Jesus. The more they tried to restrain him from shouting, the more he halal the name of the Lord and eventually, he caught the undivided attention of Jesus Christ as he passed by. Although they are many voices out there that would want to stop your worship and your praise like they tried to do to blind Bartimaeus, you have to be equally determined not to give in to any voices of opposition to your worship.

The devil will try to stop your worship by throwing all he can at you but the devil can't stop a true worshipper from worshipping their God. That's why God picks the worshipper from obscurity and elevates them unto high places, simply because they will worship him. God forbid my body may be ailing and I may be sick to the point of death, but even in my sick bed I will bless the Lord at all times, and His praise shall continually be in my mouth.

Chapter Five

PRAISE GOD IN HIS SANCTUARY

Psalm 150:1b.

This chapter will be drawn from the second clause of Psalm 150:1, ***"PRAISE GOD IN HIS SANCTUARY"***.

The first clause of Psalm 150:1, *(Praise ye the Lord),* tells us "How to praise God" and, the second clause *(Praise God in His sanctuary),* tells us where to praise Him. Hence the sphere of praise is in His sanctuary, and by His Saints on earth. This clause has to do with earthly worship because it is worship rendered by mortals and other earthly creation.

Just consider this; If you begin to Halal God in the subway or in the shopping Mall in the way he ought to be praised in accordance with Psalm 150:1a, chances are you may be arrested by security and charged for disturbing public peace.

If you try to *Halal* him in the office setting or in a corporate environment, chances are that your employer may either get rid of you for reason of insanity or at the minimum, have you fired from the job for using your employer's time to engage in the private practice of your faith.

Even worse than that is attempting to praise God loudly at the top of your voice in a mental health institution. Before you know it, you will be restrained, injected with a tranquilizer and considered a mentally ill patient.

And so the Psalmist in Psalm 150:1b takes the time to tell us how it should be done and where praises ought to be rendered unto God. That is in the sanctuary of our God.

> True worship is not an act. It is an encounter, the experience with God's presence.

When you see people worshipping God in church, in a way that may seem crazy to you, you just have to allow them because they are doing it in the right place. This is where God ought to be praised according to the Psalmist. So be careful not to despise or criticize people simply because they are praising God in a manner that seem unusual to you.

For all you know, sometimes people need to praise God the way they do just so they will stay sane and not lose their minds. You don't know what some people go home to when they leave church or the nature of the circumstances that some people have to deal with on daily basis. So, when they come into God's presence, it's their only opportunity to get it all out of their system, whatever they may have endured through the course of the day or week. Besides, they are simply doing what the bible says we should do anyway and that is to praise God in His Sanctuary.

So the second clause commands us to; "Praise God in His Sanctuary".

Now, the question then is; Who is this God that the Psalmist is referring to in Psalm 150:1b?

One of the earliest and most primitive references to God is by the Hebrew word 'EL'. The word EL is from an ancient description of God which means;

1) The strong one or to be exact, the all-powerful and all-mighty One.

EL,–is actually part of the Hebrew words *Elohim* or *El-Shaddai.*

El-Shaddai, on the other hand, has a very interesting meaning because it comes from the two Hebrew words 'EL' and 'Shaddai'.

EL means the Strong One and Shaddai is the Hebrew word for breast. Hence putting the two together, El-Shaddai therefore means the "the strong breasted One." This description of God is interesting because, when you think about God as the El-Shaddai, you could also think of him in the light of a mother breast feeding her baby.

Modern day science has proven over and over again that babies sustained on the breast are normally healthier than those fed on the bottle. Not only are they healthier, but researchers has proven that they feel more secure than their counterparts who are fed on the bottle. That is why it's common for medical practitioners to strongly recommend that mothers develop the habit of breast feeding their babies instead of the use of the bottle.

So to Halal God is not just about shouting out some words of praise and adoration unto God, but also it is the acknowledgement of the fact that the All-mighty God unto whom we render our praise is He who abundantly feeds us with the unlimited resources of His breast. Hence, when we praise God, we are praising the "breasted One" not just for his provision, but also because he makes us secure in all spheres of our being and existence.

Our mothers will tell you that breastfeeding as we know it, demands the full attention of the mother. A mother cannot breast feed her baby while doing the laundry or washing the dishes at the same time. Breastfeeding is an activity that demands the undivided attention of a mother. Hence when breast feeding the baby, the mother would usually have to stop all she is doing in order to give the baby her undivided attention.

God is more concern about our
'Wholeness' than he is about our
physical healing.

If you notice carefully, it's usually during the process of breast-feeding that the mother would take a keen look at her baby by turning the baby around to make sure that the diapers are not wet. It is during this time that mothers would usually feel the baby out, check inside the ears, raise the arms and examine the legs and other parts of the baby to ensure that the baby is growing right and that there are no developmental issues with the baby.

The strong breasted one (El-Shaddai)
does not only provide for our needs,
but also checks us out to see what
else may be lacking in our lives that
needs his undivided attention.

In like manner, that is exactly what the El-Shaddai; (the mighty breast-feeding One) does to the believer when attending to our needs. First and foremost, God gives us His full and undivided attention since he is the El-Shaddai. Not only does the El-Shaddai feeds the believer by supplying his or her needs, but while he is attending to our needs, just like the mother feeding her baby, God also check us out to see what else might be happening or going on in our lives that requires his undivided attention. He turns us around in his everlasting arms, rubs us over to examine the state of our well-being and ensure that we are not just fine but made 'whole'.

When God, the El-Shaddai touches the believer, he touches our being as a whole and not only some aspects of our being. That's why at the pool of Bethesda, Jesus did not ask the impotent man who had been lying around for 38 years whether he wished to the healed. Rather, Jesus asked him if he wanted to be made 'whole'. There is a big difference between being healed of an infirmity and being made whole. Being healed, ministers to the physical body, whiles being made 'whole' attends to the whole well-being of a person. This includes the person's physical healing as well as the mental, psychological, social, and spiritual well-being of the person.

> To be made 'whole' is not limited to your physical healing, but also addresses our mental, social, and spiritual wellness.

Whiles the water that the impotent man was waiting to jump into for the past 38 years could only minister to his physical impotency, Jesus the El-Shaddai, saw beyond the physical needs of the impotent man. He therefore offered him an option that was all-inclusive and far better than what the healing powers of the pool could offer.

God always sees beyond our needs and provides us with what we really need in other to be made whole. That is why the scriptures declares that even in our asking of him, we know not what to pray for, but the Spirit makes intercession for us with groaning that cannot be uttered. Isn't that amazing? that even in our making of requests for our needs, the El-Shaddai intercedes on our behalf just so we would in his presence be made 'whole'.

The fact is that one may be healed of his or her physical impediment, only to go home from a hospital, a rehabilitation center, therapy, or even prison only to have to deal with many other issues associated with ones' psychological, social, or mental well-being. At times, some of these issues are even bigger and more challenging to deal with than the physical impediment from which one was delivered from.

This impotent man had been out of mainstream society for 38 years and that's a lifetime because for an example, if he was 2 years old when he became a resident of the pool at Bethesda, he would be 40 years old at the time of his healing. If he was for an example a married adult when he went to the pool, who knows if his wife would have had the patience to wait on him all these 38 years, not to mention the well-being of his children if any.

And so Jesus, in his capacity as the El-Shaddai, saw far beyond the impotent man's physical needs and impediments and offered him 'wholeness' instead of just a physical correction of his impediment. That is simply what the El-Shaddai does to every child of his who goes to him for attention of any sort.

At times, people are deceived by the enemy to think that their accomplishments are as a result of their smartness or hard work. Don't be fooled into thinking for a second, that you are where you are today because of your hard work. There are people who work ten times harder than you, yet they are far behind where you are today.

According to the Psalmist "My soul is escaped as a bird out of the snare of the fowlers: the snare is broken, and we are escaped. [8] Our help is in the name of the Lord, who made heaven and earth." Psalm 124:7-8

Some people are walking-miracles because despite the fact that parts of your bodies are held together by chicken wires and by the insecure and unguaranteed medical procedures of doctors, yet they are still alive because they are being sustained in the arms of the Al-mighty breasted-one, the El-Shaddai.

And so when you come to the understanding that you have the undivided attention of El-Shaddai and that you are under his gracious scrutiny 24/7–it should make you want to open your mouth, raise your hands and Halal Yah for his goodness towards you. That is why every time we have the opportunity to come before God's presence, whether in our private closet or in a congregational setting, we owe him the best of our worship, the best of our praise, the best of our adoration and the best of our offering unto his holy name. When I consider the goodness of the Lord, and all that he has done for me, anything offered to God that is short of the best is an insult to His name. That's why the Psalmist declared that;

"What shall I render unto the Lord for all his benefits towards me? I will take my cup of salvation, and call upon the name of the Lord." **Psalm 116:12-13.**

To conclude this chapter; I would like to say that the reason why we are instructed by the Psalmist to praise God in His sanctuary is because His sanctuary is a place within our reach. You will discover in the next chapter that there are other places as well that God ought to be praised which are beyond the reach of mortals.

Chapter Six

PRAISE HIM IN THE FIRMAMENT OF HIS POWER

Psalm 150:1c

I n this third part of Psalm 150:1, the Psalmist now suggests something else after telling us how and where to Halal Yah. The Psalmist here suggests that Praising God should not be limited only to God's Sanctuary but also it should be done in the firmament of God's power. Hence unlike the preceding clause, the sphere of praise according to Psalm 150:1c is "in the firmament of His power". Note that this has to do with celestial worship because it is outside the realm of humans and earthly creation.

Now, this is interesting because of the meaning of the word firmament. The word firmament means the visible arch of the sky or the visible blues of the sky. The word firmament has its roots from the story of creation in the book of Genesis.

In the book of Genesis, we are told; "And God said, Let there be a firmament in the midst of the waters, and let it divide the waters from the waters. [7] And God made the firmament, and divided the waters which were under the firmament from the waters which were above the firmament: and it was so. [8] And God called the firmament Heaven. And the evening and the morning were the second day. [9] And God said, Let the waters under the heaven be gathered together unto one place, and let the dry land appear: and it was so". **Genesis 1:6-9**

Firmament = from the Hebrew *"raw-kee-ah"*
Meaning   1) An extended surface.
                   2) Of a vault of heaven supporting
                        waters above.

The reason why the command to praise God in the firmament of his power is an interesting proposal is because this realm is obviously beyond the reach of humans or mortals. So, the question then becomes; how can this be accomplished if indeed the firmament is out of the reach of man?

This literally means that the praises of our God is not limited to the earth or to the earthly sanctuary alone, but rather, it goes beyond the physical realm of human existence and extends to another realm that is not reachable to mankind. That realm is the visible arch of the sky, referred to as the firmament.

Since men obviously don't live in the sky or in the visible arch of the sky, to whom then is the Psalmist referring when he commands that God should be praised in the exterior-blue of the sky? Also, it is worth noting that in the firmament (or in the exterior blue of the sky), God ought to be praised (halal) according to His power and mighty works. This is obviously referring to God's work in creation and redemption.

This also means that God should be praised for His ability to enforce His will over all things both in heaven and on earth.

- In the book of Daniel , we are told; "***God does what He wills, and no man can question him and say "why doest thou this?"*** **Daniel 4:35b**
- In the book of Isaiah we are told that, ***"Who hath directed the Spirit of the Lord, or being his Counselor hath taught him? With whom took he counsel, and who instructed him, and taught him in the path of judgment, and taught him, and showed to him the way of understanding?*** **Isaiah 40:13-14.**

In other words, no one tells him what to do or how it ought to be done.

- In the book of Job, we are told that *"When he giveth quietness, who then can make trouble? And when he hideth his face, who then can behold him..."* **Job 34:29**

And so, this El-Shaddai, this All-existing and All-sufficient one, possesses all the power and the ability to do whatsoever He will and no one in heaven and on earth can question or challenge him.

God therefore ought to be praised (*Halal*) in the firmament of His power because when it comes to God's power, the praise ascribed to His power ought to be done in heaven since in heaven dwells His throne. The throne of God is where decisions are made, because a king always declares His will from his throne.

Therefore, the answer to the question about who should praise Him in the firmament of His power could be found in the fourth chapter of the book of Revelation. This command according to Revelation 4:4 is referring to the Angels in heaven and other creatures that are found as well in Heaven.

What this means therefore is that what we do here on earth when we are praising God, is not limited to the earth because we are following a pattern that already exists in Heaven. I will prove this to you in a moment. Just as the temple of old was a prototype of what exists in heaven, so is the temple of praise and worship a prototype of what goes on in heaven.

The only difference being that heavens' praise is non-stop; it is eternal and goes on without a break, while earthly praise is obviously subject to constraint in terms of time and space which is typical of the realm of mankind.

Revelation 4:4 gives us a preview as to what's happening in Heaven and what praising God looks like in Heaven.

> *⁴ And round about the throne were four and twenty seats: and upon the seats I saw four and twenty elders sitting, clothed in white raiment; and they had on their heads crowns of gold.*
> *⁶ And before the throne there was a sea of glass like unto crystal: and in the midst of the throne, and round about the throne, were four beasts full of eyes before and behind.*
> *⁷ And the first beast was like a lion, and the second beast like a calf, and the third beast had a face as a man, and the fourth beast was like a flying eagle.*
> *⁸ And the four beasts had each of them six wings about him; and they were full of eyes within: and they rest not day and night, saying,*

Holy, holy, holy, Lord God Almighty, which was, and is, and is to come.
⁹ And when those beasts give glory and honor and thanks to him that sat on the throne, who liveth for ever and ever,
¹⁰ The four and twenty elders fall down before him that sat on the throne, and worship him that liveth for ever and ever, and cast their crowns before the throne, saying,
¹¹ Thou art worthy, O Lord, to receive glory and honor and power: for thou hast created all things, and for thy pleasure they are and were created.
Revelation4:4, 6-11

In Revelation 4:4, we are told that round about the throne of God are twenty and four seats and upon it are seated the twenty-four elders clothe in white raiment with crowns of gold on their heads. Note that the passage will later on reveal the purpose for the crowns on their heads of these heavenly creatures and what it is meant to be used for. These twenty-four elders are great men who ascended into heaven in their resurrected bodies.

In verse 7 of the same chapter, we are told that also around about the throne are four beasts full of eyes inside them. The first is like a lion, the second like a calf, the third had a face of man and the fourth is like a flying eagle. These are symbolic representation of the four gospels in the New Testament. It's worth noting that these four living creatures mentioned in the book of revelation were first revealed to the Prophet Ezekiel in Ezekiel chapter 1, thousands of years before John had his revelation on the island of Patmos.

The 8th verse further tells us that each of the four beasts is full of eyes inside of them. Eyes in the bible, signifies insight or the ability to obtain information. This is so because since they are in close proximity to the throne of God, they have access to information that you and I don't have access to.

What information would this be, one may ask? They have information about;

i) The will of God
ii) The decisions of God
iii) The divine purpose of God

CELESTIAL WORSHIP

And so what is the nature of worship as it is done in heaven? The bible declares that: day & night, these creatures did nothing but to praise and worship God. What this means is that, in heaven, the Halal (praise) is a continuous action and event that never ceases. While here on earth, we are told to praise God in the sanctuary and after that we go home to occupy ourselves with other cares of this life, in heaven the praise and worship around the throne of God does not stop. It goes on continuously and eternally without a pause or break in worship and adoration unto Him who sits on the throne.

"Worship on earth is a prototype of
the non-stop worship that goes on
in Heaven"

One may be curious to know what these eternal worshippers are saying or singing out as they render praises unto God. What is it that these creatures are saying that may or may not be different from what we humans say when praising God on earth? The answer to this question is no secret because the bible tells us exactly what they are saying as they worship before the throne of God. According to Revelation 4; 8 night and day; they worship him who sat upon the throne saying;

HOLY...HOLY...HOLY
And that is followed by another group saying;
LORD GOD ALMIGHTY
And then follows yet another group saying;
WHICH WAS, AND IS, AND IS TO COME

This is interesting to me because in my studies, I found out that 'holy' in the Hebrew language means 'different'. So that being the case, what these celestial worshippers are saying to God in worship is that God is different or distinct from all else that exist. Indeed he is totally different from all else. The book of Hebrew makes us to understand that

God is different from Abraham. He is different from Moses; He is different from the Aaronic priesthood, and different from all others who ever represented Him throughout the ages. Hence, it's no surprise that these celestial worshippers are proclaiming God as being distinct from all else in their worship round about the throne of God.

THE WORSHIP OF KINGS

In my wildest imagination of how worship will be around the throne of God, I feel a chill all over my body. Notice that in verse 10 of Revelation chapter 4, something unique began to happen in the midst of all these continuous praise, worship and adoration round about the throne. Remember that earlier in this chapter, I made mentioned of the fact that the crowns that the celestial worshippers had on their heads was for a specific purpose.

In the New Testament there are two Greek synonyms for the word 'crown' and both words are connected to the word *basilikos* which means royal. The first word is *'diadema'* which means a crown as a badge of royalty. For example, a kingly element made to be worn on the head. The second word is *'Stephanos'* which is a crown in the sense of a wreath or of badge of victory in games or civic worth.

Crown is used in the bible figuratively and symbolically. By their nature, crowns are symbols of honor and indications of high level of performance in any condition under which they are awarded.

The bible declares that **"our labor in Christ shall not be in vain".** If so, then what shall we get in return for our labor in the Lord? According to I Corinthians 3:14; we will have rewards according to the degree of our labor in the Lord.

> *[14] If any man's work abide which he hath built thereupon, he shall receive a reward.* **I Corinthians 3:14**

These rewards will be in the form of crowns. At least six different types of crowns have been identified in the New Testament as the reward for believers who would success-fully endure to the end.

TYPES OF CROWN
1) THE IMPERISHABLE CROWN / CROWN INCORRUPTIBLE
This crown is for those who have led others to Christ. (1 Cor. 9:25)
2) THE CROWN OF LIFE
This crown is for those who success-fully endure trails and persecutions of their faith. (James 1:12)
3) THE CROWN OF RIGHTEOUSNESS
This type of crown awaits those who love the appearance of Christ (maranatha– Lord come quickly–2 Tim 4:8)
4) THE CROWN OF GLORY

91

This is a never-ending share of glory a crown given by the chief Shepherd (Jesus Christ), to the faithful shepherds of the body of Christ which is the church. (1 Peter 5:4)

5) THE CROWN OF REJOICING

This is also a crown for those who labor in bringing others to Christ. God respects those who labor faithfully in Him so others will be born into the kingdom. (I Thessalonians 2:19)

6) THE CROWN OF THORNS.

Above all the other crowns listed above, the crown of thorns is one that is inevitable to the life of the believer. One cannot possess any of the above listed crowns unless they first put on the "crown of thorns". This is what Jesus referred to in Luke 9:23 when He declared that; *"if any man will come after me, let Him deny himself and take up **His cross** daily and follow me."*

Notice that reference is made not to the cross of Christ but rather to the believer's personal cross (His cross). The cross symbolizes suffering for the sake of Christ and the gospel. It is personalized in the above scripture because every child of God has his or her own cross to bear. Our faith experiences and challenges are unique for every believer. The challenges that Jesus had to endure in the flesh as the savior of mankind is different from our challenges and our challenges and temptations are unique from that of each other; beside the fact that our challenges are on a daily basis.

The Apostle Paul in his exhortation to the church at Philippi presented in a similar fashion as Jesus did, the following; ***"...that I may know him in the power of his resurrection, and in the fellowship (sharing) of his suffering, being made conformable unto his death." (Philippians 3:10)***

THE PURPOSE OF THE CROWNS

According to Revelation 4:10, regardless of what type of crown the believer is awarded with, the sole purpose would be to be used in the worship of the King of Kings and the Lord of Lords. Since He is King of Kings, those who will have the privilege to worship Him, first ought to be crowned kings. Notice that in the midst of the worship in heaven, the bearers of the crowns cast down their crowns in adoration to Him that sat upon the throne.

The sole purpose for the believer's crown in heaven will be to be used in worshiping the King of Kings and the Lord of Lords.

Even in His death, it was necessary that Jesus would be crowned as the Kingly savior or redeemer of mankind. This is a mystery because Jesus really required a crown on the cross to qualify Him as the chief sinner.

Therefore, it was not by chance or by accident that the Roman Soldiers would plate a crown of thorns to over His head.

In the minds of the Roman Soldiers, it was perceived as a mockery and an object of torture, but in the plan of God, it was a seal of approval that indeed Jesus came to die as a chief sinner in the place of all sinners. What physically identify one as a King is the crown. The crown of thorns was to affirm the fact that although a King, He made himself of no reputation so He will be the propitiation for the sins of mankind. This was done so the scripture would be fulfilled as it is written;

"For he hath made him to be sin for us, who knew no sin, that we might be made the righteousness of God in him." Corinthians 5:21

Notice that according to the 10th verse: The twenty and four Elders then threw themselves on the ground before the throne, cast down their crowns and also joined in the worship saying; according to the verse 11 **"Thou art worthy, O Lord, to receive glory and honor and power: for thou hast created all things, and for thy pleasure they are and were created."**

This is not the kind of worship that is known on earth because on earth, it is the king's subjects who worships and honors a king, but in heaven it takes a crowned King to worship and honor the King of Kings. This is what I call *"the worship of Kings"*, since God is the King of Kings, only Kings can worship before His presence. This therefore means that if we are given the privilege to worship God on earth, it's only because we are also Kings in the earthly realm of affairs. Worship, whether on earth or in heaven, is therefore a privilege for Kings only.

This makes God rightfully the King of kings however, it also places the worshipper in the position of a crowned King. So when we make reference to God as the King of Kings, it means His worshippers have to be King themselves in order to qualify them to wor-ship him regardless of whether the worship is rendered unto him on earth or in heaven. So when you are instructed to Halal him, it's simply because you are yourself a King.

Just as it takes principalities to fight prin-cipalities, and powers to fight powers, so does it take Kings to worship the King of Kings. Therefore, lay aside your pride and join in the universal symphony to worship the King of Kings and the Lord of Lords, because this is not an ordinary worship. It is the worship rendered by Kings unto the King of Kings.

Chapter Seven

CONCLUSION
THE UNIVERSAL SYMPHONY

"Let everything that hath breath praise the Lord"

Dictionary.com defines the word 'symphony' as "anything characterized by a harmonious combination of elements, especially as in an effective combination of musical notes."

THE INSTRUMENTS OF MUSIC

In order to emphasize the universality of praise, various instruments of music are employed in the praise of God according to Psalm 150:1-6. In verses 3-6, the Psalmist instructs the worshipper to praise God on the following instruments of music; the harp, the psaltery, the timbrel, string instrument and the sounding cymbal, etc. The goal of praising

God on the various instruments of music I believe is to create a universal symphony.

It seem like these instruments were the major instruments employed in the making of music in the old Jewish traditional setting. The horn was the curved "Shophar," blown by the priests; the "<u>harp</u> and <u>psaltery</u>" were played by the Levites. Timbrels were played by women as noted in the 'exodus praise' when Miriam, the sister of Moses led the women in praise with the sound of the timbrel. Furthermore, dancing, the playing on stringed instruments and pipes and cymbals, were not reserved for the Levites. "Pipe" is probably that used by shepherds, hence the summons to praise God is addressed to Priests, Levites, and all people irrespective of their race, gender or vocation.

As mentioned in the earlier chapters, "Praise Ye the Lord" is an all-inclusive command. Unlike "thou" which refers to one person, "ye" as mentioned before means you, or all of you, meaning the command to praise the Lord is not negotiable. Whether you want to or not, whether you're white or black or Indian or rich or poor or educated or uneducated everyone has the duty to glorify God in praise and worship unto him. Hence it's not a surprise that the Psalmist lists different instruments which are traditionally played by different classes of people within the old Jewish culture. That in itself reveals the encompassing nature of worship.

THE UNIVERSAL SYMPHONY

From the long list of musical instruments listed in this Psalm, one would expect that each instrument took part in the liturgical worship within ancient Jewish culture, till at last all sounds from the various instruments of music blended in a mighty torrent of praiseful sound.

As if that is not enough, the Psalmist also calls on "everything that hath breath" to use it in sending forth a thunder chorus of praise to Jehovah. This is in strange contrast to modern day notions of sobriety in worship where people come into the presence of God and sit still like Egyptian mummies or simply act like spectators in that, although they are present, they are also disengaged in the worship experience of the church.

One would notice that throughout the last five psalms (i.e. Psalm. 146–Psalm 150), also referred to as the halallic Psalms, from the Hebrew praise word Halal one would discover that there are 'no wails of penitence', but rather on the contrary, a heightening tone of jubilant and adoring praise. These praises of God, builds up momentum beginning gradually from the first halallic Psalm in Psalm 146 until it culminates in the last verse of the last chapter of the book of Psalms.

"I cannot sing, nor can I play, and speech is inadmissible, does not disqualify you from praising the Lord, provided you can breathe"

The melody of which even swells higher and louder until it reaches its climax in the "doxology" or what is known as the "hallelujah chorus" of the book of Psalm where the Psalmist demands a universal outburst of adoration. As a result, he summoned in the last verse of the last chapter for "everything that hath breath to join in the grand oratorio".

The expression; "Let every breath you breathe praise the Lord" signifies the inclusion of all creatures without reservation. Thus rendered, it is an extensive appeal addressed to the universe, including all that dwell in the waters, and all creatures in the air and all creatures in terrestrial habitats. The implication here is that; all creatures, which after the disunion and disorder caused by sin have been removed, are now harmoniously united for a universal choral.

In addition, the chorus of mankind concerting with the angelic chorus are become one cymbal of divine praise, and the final song of victory which will salute God, the triumphant Conqueror and everlasting King of Kings with shouts of non-stop adoration.

This summon to a universal symphony, does not comprise of the earthly human worshippers and the celestial or angelic worshippers alone. It also applies to all creation that has the God-giving ability to breathe. This therefore includes all species of the animal kingdom as well as all species of the plant kingdom since plants also have breath.

One may think of it this way; a worshipper may say when thinking of the service of praise and his own limitations, "I cannot sing, nor can I play, and speech is inadmissible." "granted," replies the psalmist, "but you can breathe"; and so the implication here is that if the vocal and the instrumental be denied you, having your breath still qualifies you to join in this universal symphony to render praise unto Him to whom all praise is due.

From this conclusion, one would understand that the Psalmist is being very careful in Psalm 150, in his command for all life to praise the Lord because, we have talents unequal, and gifts unequal. However, breath is the only factor of equality for all life whether it is humans, animals or plants. What we all have in common therefore, and for which no living thing can claim a disadvantage is breath. Hence the command;

"Let every thing that hath breath praise the LORD. Praise ye the Lord."

O' what a thrilling crash of melody! What a volume of perfect harmony, when all animate and inanimate creation, with all creatures, rising rank upon rank, order above order, species above species, purged from corruption and delivered from all evil, shall join in one harmonious universal symphony to crown God Lord of all creation at the command for everything that hath breath to praise the LORD–Praise ye the Lord.

LIST OF REFERENCES

1. *(Collins English Dictionary–Complete & Unabridged 2012 Digital Edition)© William Collins Sons & Co. Ltd. 1979, 1986 © Harper Collins Publishers 1998, 2000, 2003, 2005, 2006, 2007, 2009, 2012*
2. *JPS Tanakh 1917. Hallelujah. The Holy Scriptures according to the Masoretic Text. Jewish Publication Society.*
3. *Pastor Victor T. Nyarko's sermon notes (2003-2014) – From Sermons preached at Victory Family Worship Center and other venues.*
4. *Wesley's Notes on the Bible*
5. *Cambridge Bible for Schools and Colleges*
6. *Synopsis of the Books of the Bible, by John Nelson Darby [1857-62].*
7. *The Geneva Bible Translation Notes [1599]*
8. *John Calvin's Commentaries. Text Courtesy of <u>Christian Classics Etherial Library</u>.*

9. *Expositions of Holy Scripture, Alexander MacLaren. Text Courtesy of BibleSupport.com.*

10. *Synopsis of the Books of the Bible, by John Nelson Darby [1857-62]. Text Courtesy of Internet Sacred Texts Archive.*

11. *Biblical Commentary on the Old Testament, by Carl Friedrich Keil and Franz Delitzsch [1857-78]. Text Courtesy of Internet Sacred Texts Archive.*

12. *Young's Literal Translation*